NAVIGATING THE FINANCIAL CYCLE:

STRATEGIES FOR PROSPERITY AND RESILIENCE

MORTON J. FISHER

Contents

Contents

Introduction

The world of finance is a complex and dynamic terrain, influenced by a continual ebb and flow known as the financial cycle. Just as the tides of the ocean rise and fall, economies and markets have phases of growth, peak, contraction, and trough. This repetitive pattern determines the fate of countries, corporations, and people, bringing opportunities and difficulties in equal measure.

In "Navigating the Financial Cycle: Strategies for Prosperity and Resilience," we begin on a journey to uncover the complexity of this cycle and equip ourselves with the information and skills to make educated financial choices. Whether you're a seasoned investor, a corporate leader, or just someone seeking a deeper understanding of economic cycles, this book provides essential lessons that transcend time and situation.

We will dig into the many stages of the financial cycle, exploring the telltale indications that announce each change. From the high days of expansion, typified by rapid development and limitless optimism, to the depths of a trough, when recovery and rebuilding take center stage, we will study how these periods impact our economic environment.

Understanding the driving dynamics behind the financial cycle is crucial. We will explore the various elements that determine its course, from macroeconomic data to the choices taken by central banks and governments. By having a broad understanding of these factors, we may better predict fluctuations in the cycle and position ourselves for success.

No less significant are the methods we employ throughout each phase. In times of expansion, we will find ways to harness the promise of development while limiting hazards. As peaks approach, we will learn to control excitement and safeguard our profits. During contractions, we will dig into the art of financial resilience, making sensible decisions in the face of difficulty. And in the troughs, we will examine how to emerge stronger, harnessing the lessons of the past to construct a more secure future.

Throughout this book, we will draw from historical case studies that show the repercussions of heeding—or ignoring—the signs of the financial cycle. By exploring the Roaring Twenties and the ensuing Great Depression, the dot-com boom of the early 2000s, and the reverberations of the 2008 global financial crisis, we will find key insights that act as guideposts for today's financial environment.

Yet the financial cycle is not solely a consequence of rational economic processes. It is also intricately interwoven with human behavior, psychology, and emotions. We will investigate the interesting area of behavioral finance, diving into the biases and instincts that may lead to both extraordinary accomplishments and disastrous failures in financial decision-making.

As we peek into the future, we will analyze the revolutionary influence of technology on the financial cycle. The development of fintech, the promise of blockchain, the mysterious realm of cryptocurrencies, and the power of artificial intelligence all have the ability to transform the way we engage with markets and economies.

Ultimately, "Navigating the Financial Cycle" is a call to embrace financial awareness, resilience, and adaptation. By knowing the cycles of the financial world, we can make educated decisions that increase our own well-being and contribute to the greater prosperity of our nations. As we start on this adventure, let us equip ourselves with information, strategy, and a persistent determination to master the art of managing the financial cycle.

Understanding the Financial Cycle: A Primer

The financial cycle, much like the natural cycles of the seasons, is a recurrent pattern that changes the economic landscape. At its foundation, the financial cycle symbolizes the regular growth and contraction of economic activity, touching everything from employment and investment to consumer purchasing and market performance. In this primer, we will dig into the main ideas and components that constitute the financial cycle and lay the foundation for our analysis of its stages and repercussions.

1. The Essence of the Financial Cycle:

At its essence, the financial cycle embodies the cyclical pattern of economic development and downturn. Just as a rising tide lifts all boats, a flourishing economy generates prosperity throughout diverse industries. However, periods of unregulated expansion may lead to excesses and imbalances, finally terminating in a contraction phase when issues emerge.

2. The Four Phases of the Financial Cycle:

The financial cycle includes four widely characterized phases:

- **Expansion**: This is a time of rapid economic expansion, defined by growing GDP, increased consumer spending, and high levels of confidence. Investments and asset prices tend to grow during this time.

- **Peak**: As the growth approaches its apex, warning signs may develop. Speculative behavior and excitement might lead to asset bubbles. A peak frequently precedes a phase of contraction.

- **Contraction**: Also known as a downturn or recession, this phase entails a slowdown in economic activity. Unemployment may grow, consumer spending may drop, and companies may encounter difficulty.

- **Trough**: The trough indicates the lowest point of the cycle. During this phase, recuperation occurs, leading to resumed development and the ultimate shift back to an expansion phase.

3. Indicators and Factors:

A multitude of indicators give insights into the present phase of the financial cycle. These may include GDP growth rates, inflation levels, unemployment rates, and consumer confidence indices. Additionally, central banks have a major role in affecting the cycle via monetary policy actions, particularly interest rate changes.

4. Duration and Variability:

The length of each phase may vary greatly, driven by variables such as government policy, technical advancements, and global events. While the financial cycle is a recurrent pattern, its exact timing and features may be impossible to anticipate with full confidence.

5. Interplay with Human Behavior:

Human psychology and behavior play a key role in determining the business cycle. During moments of growth, optimism may lead to overconfidence and excessive risk-taking. Conversely, anxiety and risk aversion generally prevail during contractions, hurting investment choices and economic activity.

6. A Roadmap for the Journey Ahead:

This introduction serves as a guide for our investigation of the financial cycle. In the chapters that follow, we will go further into each phase, studying ways for managing the hurdles and capitalizing on the possibilities given by the ever-turning wheel of the financial cycle.

As we begin on this path of knowledge, let us bear in mind that a deep grasp of the financial cycle gives us the skills to make educated choices, limit risks, and position ourselves for success. Whether you are an investor, a company leader, or someone seeking a deeper knowledge of economic dynamics, the insights obtained from grasping the financial cycle will definitely be helpful.

Chapter One

The Economic Phases of the Financial Cycle

The financial cycle is a dynamic and ever-changing succession of economic stages, each marked by particular trends, behaviors, and consequences. These stages represent the natural ebb and flow of economic activity and play a key role in molding the fortunes of countries, organizations, and people. In this part, we will analyze each of the four economic stages that form the financial cycle: Expansion, Peak, Contraction, and Trough.

1. Expansion: The Era of Growth and Opportunity

Characteristics: During the expansion period, countries see significant growth in GDP, low unemployment, and growing consumer confidence. Business investment and consumer spending tend to grow, leading to a spike in economic activity. Financial markets typically perform well, and asset values increase.

Opportunity: This phase gives enterprises the opportunity to grow, invest, and innovate. Investors may profit from growing asset prices, while consumers enjoy enhanced employment opportunities and higher spending power.

2. Peak: The Pinnacle of Optimism and Caution

Characteristics: As the growth continues, optimism may lead to excessive behaviors, including speculative investments and asset bubbles. The peak period is defined by high levels of economic activity and asset values. However, warning indications, such as unsustainable debt levels or excessive risk-taking, may develop.

Cautionary Measures: Prudent investors and policymakers begin to exhibit prudence during the peak period. They may make efforts to decrease risk exposure, diversify portfolios, and constantly monitor indications that might warn of an imminent recession.

3. Contraction: Navigating the Downturn and Challenges

Characteristics: The contraction phase, sometimes referred to as a recession or downturn, entails a drop in economic activity. Unemployment grows, consumer spending slows down, and companies may suffer. Financial markets may endure dips, and asset values might tumble.

Challenges and Responses: During this period, organizations may need to undertake cost-cutting measures, and people may experience job losses or income cutbacks. Effective fiscal and monetary policies are vital to supporting economic recovery and restoring confidence.

4. Through Rebuilding and Preparing for Recovery

Characteristics: The trough phase symbolizes the lowest point of the cycle when economic activity stabilizes and begins to rebound. Unemployment may peak, but hints of recovery appear. Consumer morale continues to recover, and firms cautiously restart investments.

Recovery Strategies: Governments and central banks typically employ stimulus measures to aid recovery. Savvy investors and companies discover opportunities to position themselves for development, such as by purchasing undervalued assets or expanding operations.

These four phases are not discrete occurrences but rather interrelated stages that constantly flow into one another. Just as winter yields to spring and summer transitions to fall, the financial cycle's phases affect and pave the way for future stages.

Recognizing the signals of each phase and knowing the methods that fit with them is vital for making educated financial choices and efficiently traversing the varied terrain of the financial cycle.

Expansion: Growth, Opportunities, and Exuberance

The expansion phase of the financial cycle is characterized by thriving economic growth, plentiful possibilities, and a feeling of enthusiasm. During this era, economies witness a rise in economic activity, and different indications hint towards a flourishing environment. Let's go more into the features and dynamics of the expansion phase:

1. Rapid Economic Growth:

GDP Expansion: Gross Domestic Product (GDP) expands at a quicker pace, indicating greater output, consumption, and investment. Businesses see growing revenues, and governments generally observe greater tax receipts.

2. Low Unemployment:

Job Creation: Employment possibilities abound as enterprises grow their operations. Unemployment rates decline, resulting in improved job stability and higher consumer expenditure.

3. Consumer Confidence and Spending:

Optimism Prevails: Consumer confidence increases, encouraging consumers to feel confident about their financial future. This optimism translates into increased levels of consumer expenditure across many industries.

4. Business Investment:

Capital Outlay: Companies commit money to develop their operations, create new goods, and invest in breakthrough technology. Business investments contribute to economic development and employment creation.

5. Stock Market Performance:

Bull Market: Financial markets tend to do well during the expansion period. Stock prices grow, and investors may receive good returns on their investments.

6. Real Estate Growth:

Property prices: Real estate markets may witness increases in property prices, driven by increasing demand for homes and commercial spaces.

7. Innovation and Entrepreneurship:

Innovation Flourishes: The climate of growth fosters entrepreneurial initiatives and the creation of new technology, goods, and services.

8. Credit Availability:

Easier Borrowing: Financial institutions frequently give easier access to credit, helping companies and individuals finance investments and expenditures.

9. Challenges and Risks:

Risk of Over-Optimism: While growth provides tremendous opportunity, there is a risk of over-optimism and complacency, which may lead to excessive risk-taking and the possible development of asset bubbles.

10. Preparing for the Next Phase:

Strategic Planning: Savvy investors and companies utilize the growth phase to prepare for the eventual transition to the next phase. They may examine portfolios, assess risk exposure, and propose measures to safeguard profits.

Peak: Optimism, Speculation, and Warning Signs

The peak phase of the financial cycle is a time marked by a culmination of economic growth, heightened confidence, and the appearance of speculative behaviors. While the atmosphere stays buoyant, warning indicators start to develop, signaling that the cycle may be reaching a tipping point. Let's analyze the dynamics and features of the peak phase:

1. Exuberant Optimism:

Elevated Confidence: Optimism about economic prospects reaches its pinnacle, leading to a general perception that the present growth track is sustainable.

2. Speculative Activities:

Asset Bubbles: Speculative behaviors and irrational enthusiasm may contribute to the emergence of asset bubbles, when the values of specific assets, such as stocks or real estate, become divorced from their underlying fundamentals.

3. High Asset Prices:

Overvaluation: The values of different assets, including stocks and real estate, may become overvalued owing to high demand fueled by speculative investment.

4. Increased Leverage:

Borrowing Abundance: Easy access to credit and low interest rates may encourage people and companies to take on larger levels of debt to fund investments and consumption

5. Market Volatility:

Swings in Prices: Financial markets face higher volatility as mood fluctuates swiftly between optimism and caution.

6. Central Bank Actions:

Monetary Policy: Central banks may start to tighten monetary policy by increasing interest rates to contain possible inflation and avoid the building of systemic concerns.

7. Potential Warning Signs:

Slowing Growth: Economic growth rates may start to slow down compared to prior eras of boom.

Margin Debt: An increase in margin debt, when investors borrow money to participate in the market, might be suggestive of excessive risk-taking.

Proliferation of Financial Products: The emergence of complicated financial products and exotic investing methods may imply a chase for larger profits without proper consideration of risk.

Inverted Yield Curve: An inverted yield curve, when short-term interest rates surpass long-term rates, might suggest investor fears about future economic prospects.

8. Prudent Caution:

Risk Assessment: Investors and companies exercise prudence by reassessing their risk exposure and examining their portfolios for possible weaknesses.

Diversification: Strategies such as portfolio diversification and the deployment of assets across multiple sectors or industries become increasingly crucial.

9. Preparing for Contraction:

Risk Management: As the peak period proceeds, people and organizations make preemptive efforts to limit possible losses during the forthcoming recession phase.

Contraction: Downturn, Challenges, and Prudent Actions

The contraction phase of the financial cycle is a hard time marked by economic slowness, lower activity, and the emergence of numerous issues. During this era, organizations, investors, and people confront severe obstacles, requiring cautious navigation and smart decision-making. Let's analyze the traits and behaviors related to the contraction phase:

1. Economic Slowdown:

GDP Contraction: Economic growth rates fall, possibly leading to negative GDP growth. It's conceivable for firms to suffer a reduction in demand for their products and services.

2. Rising Unemployment:

Job Losses: As economic activity slows, firms may save expenses by decreasing their staff, resulting in rising unemployment rates.

3. Decreased Consumer Spending:

Consumer Caution: Consumer confidence wanes, resulting in lower expenditure on discretionary products. People concentrate on the fundamentals and may postpone significant expenditures.

4. Reduced Business Investment:

Capital Constraints: Businesses become more cautious about capital expenditures, postponing growth plans and new investments.

5. Market Volatility and Declines:

Bear Market: Financial markets endure lengthy falls, frequently culminating in a bear market as stock values fall by 20% or more from their previous highs.

6. Credit Tightening:

Reduced Access: Lenders may reduce credit availability, making it more difficult for people and enterprises to get loans and funding.

7. Default Risks:

Debt Stress: The recession phase may lead to increasing default rates on loans and obligations, especially for enterprises suffering revenue issues.

8. Prudent Actions:

Cost Management: Businesses employ cost-cutting initiatives to safeguard cash flow and maintain financial stability.

Liquidity Preservation: Individuals and companies concentrate on creating or retaining adequate emergency cash to weather the economic headwinds.

Portfolio Reassessment: Investors reassess their investment portfolios, perhaps reallocating assets to safer havens or defensive positions.

Debt Reduction: Prioritizing debt reduction and avoiding new borrowings helps minimize financial hardship.

Adaptive Strategies: Entrepreneurs and business executives examine new techniques to adjust their services to shifting market circumstances.

9. Government Interventions:

Stimulus steps: Governments and central banks may execute stimulus packages to promote economic recovery, including steps to stimulate lending and boost consumer spending.

10. Positioning for Recovery:

Identifying prospects: Astute investors and forward-thinking enterprises uncover undervalued assets and growth prospects that may arise once economic circumstances stabilize.

Long-Term Planning: Using the contraction phase to strategically prepare for the ultimate recovery helps people and organizations position themselves for future development.

Trough: Recession, Recovery, and Positioning for the Future

The trough phase of the financial cycle is a key time characterized by the bottoming out of economic activity, followed by the slow process of recovery and rebuilding. As problems begin to decrease, opportunities appear for those who are prepared to profit from the inevitable upswing. Let's study the traits and techniques related to the trough phase:

1. Recession Challenges:

Economic Low Point: The trough symbolizes the lowest point of the cycle, with economic activity bottoming out. Unemployment may peak as companies continue to battle with obstacles.

2. Economic Stabilization:

Signs of Hope: Early evidence of stability may appear, such as reducing job losses and steadying company activity. These indications represent the earliest stages of healing.

3. Recovery Signals:

Gradual Improvement: As economic circumstances improve, industries may enjoy moderate growth. Consumer confidence starts to build, leading to better spending.

4. Government Support:

Stimulus Measures: Governments and central banks may continue to give assistance via targeted stimulus packages, infrastructure projects, and measures to stimulate lending.

5. Opportunistic Investments:

Undervalued Assets: Investors with a long-term view may discover chances to purchase assets at reduced prices, positioning themselves for future returns.

6. Business Adaptation:

Innovation and Efficiency: Businesses use the trough period as a time to innovate, simplify operations, and refocus their plans to suit shifting market needs.

7. Skill Development:

Upskilling: Individuals utilize the trough period to invest in education and skill development, strengthening their credentials for future work chances.

8. Financial Positioning:

Debt Management: Addressing and lowering debt loads becomes a priority, helping people and enterprises increase their financial resilience.

9. Preparation for Expansion:

Strategic Planning: Forward-thinking organizations build growth plans by researching new markets, products, or services that correspond with developing trends.

10. Long-Term Perspective:

Patience and Persistence: Recognizing that healing is a protracted process, people and organizations keep a long-term perspective while pursuing their objectives.

11. Environmental, Social, and Governance (ESG) Considerations:

Sustainable Focus: The trough period gives a chance to incorporate ESG concepts into company processes, harmonizing with increasing social and environmental demands.

12. Building Resilience:

Emergency savings: Individuals prioritize accumulating and managing emergency savings to lessen the effect of future economic crises.

Business Continuity: Organizations upgrade their business continuity strategies to better survive future interruptions.

Chapter Two
Factors Influencing the Financial Cycle

The financial cycle is driven by a complex interaction of many variables, both domestic and global, that determine economic circumstances and market dynamics. These components jointly contribute to the cyclical pattern of growth, peak, recession, and trough. Let's analyze some of the important elements that affect the financial cycle:

1. Macroeconomic Indicators:

GDP Growth: Economic growth rates have a major role in the financial cycle. Expansions are characterized by high GDP growth, whereas contractions feature reductions in economic activity.

Inflation: Changes in consumer prices and inflation rates affect buying power, interest rates, and investment decisions.

Unemployment: Labor market conditions impact consumer spending, company investment, and general economic attitude.

2. Monetary Policy:

Interest Rates: Central banks employ interest rates to impact borrowing costs, expenditure, and investment. Lower rates during contractions boost economic growth, whereas higher rates during expansions control possible overheating.

3. Fiscal Policy:

Government Spending: Fiscal policies, including government expenditures and taxation, impact demand, consumption, and investment. Stimulus methods during contractions try to promote economic activity.

4. Global Trade and Geopolitical Factors:

Trade Relations: International trade ties affect export-import dynamics, impacting economic growth and corporate performance.

Geopolitical Events: Wars, sanctions, and political instability can affect economic operations and financial markets.

5. Technological Advancements:

Innovation: Technological innovations may fuel economic development, establish new sectors, and restructure current ones, impacting employment and investment trends.

6. Financial Innovation and Regulation:

Financial Products: New financial instruments, such as derivatives and complicated securities, can create new risks and alter market behavior.

Regulatory Changes: Shifts in financial rules can alter market transparency, risk management, and investor behavior.

7. Consumer and Business Confidence:

Psychological Factors: Sentiment, expectations, and perceptions of economic circumstances impact spending, investment decisions, and market involvement

8. Global Economic Conditions:

Interconnectedness: The global economy is interconnected, and economic circumstances in one location can have rippling effects across the world.

9. Demographics:

Population Trends: Age distribution, population growth, and migration patterns impact labor force participation, consumption, and economic demand.

10. Natural Resources and Energy Prices:

Resource Scarcity: Changes in resource availability and energy prices affect production costs, inflation, and economic growth.

11. Financial Market Behavior:

Herding Behavior: Investor emotion and psychological biases can contribute to market movements, bubbles, and subsequent corrections.

12. Environmental and Climate Factors:

Climate Change: Environmental hazards, natural catastrophes, and sustainability concerns impact companies, regulations, and investments.

13. Health Crises:

Pandemics and Disease Outbreaks: Health crises can interrupt economic operations, supply networks, and consumer behavior.

Macroeconomic Indicators: GDP, Inflation, and Unemployment

Key factors termed macroeconomic indicators give perspectives on how well and effectively an economy is running. These variables have a considerable influence on how monetary policy, budgetary choices, and investment plans are established. Let's explore the relevance of GDP, inflation, and unemployment, three fundamental macroeconomic indicators.

1. Gross Domestic Product (GDP):

Definition: GDP estimates the total worth of all products and services produced within a country's boundaries during a certain time period. It is a comprehensive indication of an economy's size and performance.

Importance: GDP growth suggests economic expansion, whereas a fall signals contraction. Positive GDP growth is related to greater consumer spending, corporate investment, and job creation.

> ➤ **Phases of the Financial Cycle:**

Expansion: High GDP growth rates reflect a strong economy with increased output and consumption.

Contraction: Declining or negative GDP growth signals an economic slowdown or recession.

2. Inflation:

Definition: Inflation measures the rate at which the general price level of goods and services grows over time. It represents the decline of purchasing power and might affect consumer behavior and investment decisions.

Importance: Moderate inflation is considered beneficial for an economy, reflecting demand and economic activity. Excessive inflation can lead to lower buying power and economic instability.

➤ Phases of the Financial Cycle:

Expansion: Increasing demand during an expansion period may contribute to mild inflation.

Contraction: Economic downturns can lead to less demand, perhaps resulting in lower inflation or deflation.

3. Unemployment:

Definition: The unemployment rate represents the percentage of the labor force that is jobless and actively seeking work. It gives insights on labor market trends and general economic health.

Importance: Low unemployment suggests a vibrant job market, providing possibilities for employees. High unemployment can lead to lower consumer expenditure and economic issues.

➤ Phases of the Financial Cycle:

Expansion: Falling unemployment rates reflect a robust job market amid economic expansion.

Contraction: Rising unemployment rates are frequently symptomatic of economic issues and a contraction period.

Monetary Policy and Interest Rates

Monetary policy is a significant instrument deployed by central banks to impact the overall health and performance of an economy. It includes controlling the availability of money, credit, and interest rates to achieve certain economic goals. One of the most significant parts of monetary policy is the change in interest rates. Let's look into the relevance of monetary policy and interest rates:

1. Monetary Policy Objectives:

Price Stability: Central banks attempt to maintain steady and moderate inflation rates to minimize the erosion of buying power and foster economic certainty.

Full Employment: Central banks try to establish a level of unemployment that represents a healthy labor market while avoiding excessive joblessness.

Economic development: Monetary policy attempts to encourage sustainable economic development by affecting borrowing costs and consumer spending.

2. Interest Rates:

Definition: Interest rates are the price of borrowing money or the return on investments or savings. To impact economic activity, central banks deploy interest rates as a weapon.

➤ **Types of Interest Rates:**

Policy Rates: The central bank's official interest rates, also referred to as the benchmark or policy rates, set the tone for borrowing costs in the broader economy.

Near-Term Rates: These rates affect borrowing and lending in the near term, including consumer loans, credit cards, and short-term investments.

Long-Term Rates: Long-term rates impact borrowing for investments such as mortgages and long-term loans.

➤ **Interest Rate Changes:**

Rate Cuts: Lowering interest rates increases borrowing, investment, and consumer spending, encouraging economic development.

Rate Hikes: Raising interest rates reduces excessive borrowing, avoids overheating, and helps manage inflation.

3. Phases of the Financial Cycle:

Expansion Phase:

Low Interest Rates: Central banks frequently maintain lower interest rates to stimulate borrowing, investment, and economic development.

Peak Phase:

Rate Hikes: Central banks may raise interest rates to avoid overheating, discourage speculative tendencies, and prevent excessive inflation.

Contraction Phase:

Rate Cuts: During economic downturns, central banks decrease interest rates to encourage economic activity, boost borrowing, and assist recovery.

Trough Phase:

Accommodating Rates: Central banks continue to maintain accommodating interest rates to stimulate recovery and boost expenditure.

4.Impact on Financial Markets:

Stock Markets: As investors strive for better returns on their assets, lower interest rates may result in stronger stock market performance.

Bond Markets: Interest rate adjustments have an opposite influence on the price of bonds. Bond prices drop as rates rise, and vice versa.

Currency Markets: Interest rate variations have an influence on exchange rates, which impacts flows of international investment and trade.

5. Investment and Borrowing Decisions:

Consumer Spending: Lower interest rates might promote consumer borrowing for items like houses, vehicles, and appliances.

Business Investment: Reduced borrowing rates motivate firms to invest in expansion, equipment, and innovation.

Fiscal Policy and Government Interventions

Fiscal policy refers to the use of government expenditure and taxation to impact the economy's general health and achieve particular economic objectives. Through fiscal policy, governments may affect consumer demand, company investment, and economic growth. Let's investigate the relevance of fiscal policy and government interventions:

1. Fiscal Policy Objectives:

Economic Stimulus: Governments may raise expenditures and lower taxes during economic downturns to stimulate demand, promote consumer spending, and support corporate activity.

Budgetary Restraint: During periods of economic boom, governments may pursue policies to limit budget deficits and prevent excessive government borrowing.

2. Government Interventions:

Stimulus Measures: During economic contractions, governments can pass stimulus packages that include infrastructure projects, job development initiatives, and direct cash support for residents.

Taxation Policies: Changes in tax rates and structures can affect disposable income, consumer expenditure, and company profitability.

Public Expenditures: Investments in education, healthcare, research, and public infrastructure contribute to long-term economic growth and human capital development.

Unemployment Benefits: Providing unemployment benefits helps people and families weather economic hardships and boosts consumer spending.

3. Phases of the Financial Cycle:

Expansion Phase:

Prudent Spending: Governments may focus on preserving fiscal discipline and cutting deficits to prepare for any future downturns.

Peak Phase:

Budgetary Adjustments: As the economy hits its peak, governments may consider lowering expenditures and boosting taxes to prevent overheating and inflation.

Contraction Phase:

Stimulus Packages: Governments take fiscal measures to offer financial relief, generate employment, and promote economic activity during recessions.

Trough Phase:

Continued Support: Governments retain support measures to promote economic recovery, including targeted expenditure and investment projects.

4. Impact on Economic Activity:

Consumer Spending: Tax cuts and direct cash transfers improve disposable income, boosting consumer spending and demand.

Company Investment: Infrastructure improvements and incentives may attract company investment, leading to job creation and economic growth.

Public Services: Government expenditure on critical services and social programs helps vulnerable populations and preserves a basic level of living.

5. Budgetary Considerations:

Deficit and Debt: Fiscal policy actions can affect budget deficits and public debt levels. Prudent management tries to reconcile the need for intervention with long-term budgetary sustainability.

6. Global Economic Conditions:

Coordinated Efforts: In times of global economic crises, states may coordinate fiscal measures to accomplish collective objectives and stabilize the world economy.

7. Political and Social Factors:

Public Priorities: Government policies reflect societal values and priorities, tackling income disparity, healthcare access, education, and environmental issues.

Global Trade and Geopolitical Considerations

Global trade and geopolitical variables exert a considerable influence on the financial cycle, altering economies, markets, and investment choices. These influences transcend national borders and impact economic linkages, regulations, and market dynamics on a global scale. Let's investigate the relevance of global commerce and geopolitical considerations.

1. Global Trade Dynamics:

Trade Relationships: Bilateral and multilateral trade agreements affect the flow of products, services, and capital across borders.

Supply networks: International commerce is inextricably related to supply networks, impacting manufacturing processes, costs, and market access for enterprises.

2. Trade Policies and Tariffs:

Trade Barriers: Tariffs, quotas, and trade restrictions can disrupt trade flows, impacting pricing, demand, and profitability for exporters and importers.

Trade Liberalization: Reducing trade barriers may encourage economic growth, foster competition, and open new markets for goods and services.

3. Exchange Rates:

Currency Movements: Fluctuations in exchange rates affect the competitiveness of exports and imports, altering trade volumes and economic performance.

Trade Imbalances: Exchange rate discrepancies can lead to trade imbalances, with repercussions for trade relationships and economic stability.

4. Geopolitical Events:

Political Instability: Conflicts, regime transitions, and political tensions can impede economic operations, trade routes, and investment flows.

Sanctions: The imposition of sanctions by one government against another can hamper trade and financial activities, influencing global markets.

5. Regional Integration:

Economic Blocs: Regional trade agreements, such as the European Union or ASEAN, enable trade, investment, and economic cooperation among member nations.

6. Energy and Natural Resources:

Energy Prices: Fluctuations in oil prices affect production costs, inflation, and trade balances, particularly for energy-dependent nations.

Resource Availability: Access to the availability of natural resources impacts trade patterns and geopolitical linkages.

7. Market Access and Opportunities:

Emerging Markets: Global trade dynamics give organizations chances to enter new markets, grow client bases, and diversify income sources.

Technological Advancements: Advances in communication and transportation technology promote international commerce and extend market access.

8. Risk Assessment and Management:

Uncertainty: Geopolitical tensions and trade conflicts add uncertainty, hurting investor confidence, market sentiment, and company planning.

Hedging measures: Investors and corporations adopt risk mitigation measures such as diversification, currency hedging, and supply chain changes.

9. Multilateral Organizations:

World Trade Organization (WTO): The WTO develops global trade laws and encourages open, fair, and predictable trading practices among member nations.

International Monetary Fund (IMF): The IMF offers economic stability, financial aid, and policy coordination to meet global economic concerns.

Chapter Three

Strategies for Each Phase of the Financial Cycle

Navigating the financial cycle requires adapting strategies that align with the distinct characteristics of each phase: Expansion, Peak, Contraction, and Trough. Here are strategies tailored to each phase:

1. Expansion Phase:

Investment Diversification: Spread investments across different asset classes to manage risk and capture potential gains.

Long-Term Planning: Focus on building a solid financial foundation, saving for long-term goals, and making strategic investments.

Risk Management: Be cautious of excessive risk-taking and speculative behaviors. Balance optimism with prudent decision-making.

Skill Enhancement: Invest in education and skill development to improve employability and capitalize on growth opportunities.

2. Peak Phase:

Portfolio Reassessment: Review and rebalance investment portfolios to ensure alignment with risk tolerance and long-term objectives.

Deleveraging: Reduce debt burdens and avoid excessive borrowing to minimize financial vulnerability during potential downturns.

Defensive Positioning: Consider shifting investments toward more defensive sectors or assets that tend to perform well during economic contractions.

Emergency Fund: Strengthen emergency funds to provide a safety net during potential economic challenges.

3. Contraction Phase:

Cash Reserves: Maintain ample liquidity and cash reserves to weather income disruptions and unexpected expenses.

Cost Management: Focus on prudent spending, cut unnecessary expenses, and seek ways to reduce financial strain.

Opportunity Identification: Identify undervalued assets, potential investments, and distressed opportunities that may emerge during the downturn.

Skill Enhancement: Use downtime to acquire new skills, enhance qualifications, and prepare for the eventual recovery.

4. Trough Phase:

Strategic Investments: Consider deploying capital into assets that have been undervalued during the downturn, positioning for potential future gains.

Long-Term Vision: Maintain a patient and long-term perspective, recognizing that recovery takes time and that gradual improvement is a positive sign.

Networking and Collaboration: Connect with peers, mentors, and professionals to share insights, collaborate on projects, and explore opportunities.

Resilience Building: Focus on building financial resilience, reducing debt, and establishing a strong foundation for future economic cycles.

5. Across Phases:

Continuous Learning: Stay informed about economic trends, market dynamics, and investment opportunities to make well-informed decisions.

Adaptive Approach: Be prepared to adjust strategies based on evolving economic conditions and new information.

Emotional Discipline: Embrace disciplined decision-making and avoid succumbing to fear or overconfidence during market fluctuations.

Holistic Planning: Consider a comprehensive financial plan that encompasses savings, investments, insurance, and retirement goals.

Expansion: Capitalizing on Growth and Navigating Risks

During the expansion phase of the financial cycle, economic opportunities abound, and businesses and individuals can benefit from robust growth. However, it's important to approach this phase with a strategic mindset to capitalize on the growth while also being mindful of potential risks. Here are strategies for both capitalizing on growth and navigating risks during the expansion phase:

Capitalizing on Growth:

1. Invest in Innovation: Allocate resources to research and development to innovate products, services, and technologies that can drive growth and enhance competitiveness.

2. Expand Market Presence: Identify new markets or customer segments to expand your customer base and increase revenue streams.

3. Strategic Partnerships: Collaborate with strategic partners to leverage complementary strengths and tap into new distribution channels.

4. Business Expansion: Consider expanding operations, opening new locations, or entering new markets to seize growth opportunities.

5. Talent Acquisition: Attract top talent and invest in employee development to enhance your workforce's skills and capabilities.

6. Leverage Debt Wisely: If borrowing is necessary, use debt for productive purposes, such as expanding operations or investing in high-return projects.

Navigating Risks:

1. Risk Management Plan: Develop a comprehensive risk management plan that identifies potential risks and outlines strategies to mitigate them.

2. Diversified Portfolio: Maintain a diversified investment portfolio to spread risk across different asset classes and sectors.

3. Contingency Planning: Have contingency plans in place to address unforeseen challenges and disruptions that may arise.

4. Sustainable Growth: Avoid overexpansion that could lead to strained resources or excessive risk exposure. Focus on sustainable growth.

5. Financial Resilience: Build and maintain a healthy level of cash reserves to provide a buffer in case of unexpected downturns.

6. Monitoring Indicators: Continuously monitor economic indicators, market trends, and customer sentiment to detect early signs of potential risks.

7. Scenario Analysis: Assess how your business or investments would fare under different economic scenarios to be better prepared for various outcomes.

8. Adaptability: Remain adaptable and prepared to pivot your strategies if market conditions change unexpectedly.

Peak: Protecting Profits, Identifying Bubbles, and Reallocating Assets

As the financial cycle reaches its peak, it's essential to adopt strategies that safeguard profits, identify potential asset bubbles, and make informed decisions about reallocating assets. This phase requires a careful balance between capitalizing on remaining opportunities and preparing for potential market corrections. Here are strategies for managing your investments during the peak phase:

Protecting Profits:

1. Regular Portfolio Review: Conduct regular assessments of your investment portfolio to ensure it aligns with your financial goals and risk tolerance.

2. Profit Booking: Consider taking partial profits from investments that have experienced significant gains, locking in returns while maintaining exposure to potential further growth.

3. Trailing Stops: Implement trailing stop-loss orders to protect gains in your portfolio by automatically selling an asset if its price declines by a certain percentage from its peak.

4. Quality Focus: Prioritize high-quality, fundamentally sound investments that have strong financials and sustainable growth prospects.

5. Dividend Stocks: Consider allocating to dividend-paying stocks, which can provide a steady income stream even during market fluctuations.

Identifying Bubbles:

1. Valuation Analysis: Assess the valuation of assets to determine if they are becoming overvalued relative to their underlying fundamentals.

2. Contrarian Perspective: Maintain a contrarian mindset and avoid succumbing to herd behavior or FOMO (Fear of Missing Out) during periods of exuberance.

3. Bubble Indicators: Watch for signs of speculative behavior, rapid price increases, and excessive optimism that may indicate the formation of asset bubbles.

4. Historical Comparisons: Compare current market conditions to historical bubbles to gain insights into potential similarities and differences.

Reallocating Assets:

1. Diversification: Rebalance your portfolio to ensure diversification across different asset classes and sectors, reducing exposure to potential risks.

2. Defensive Assets: Consider reallocating a portion of your portfolio to defensive assets, such as bonds or cash equivalents, which may provide stability during market downturns.

3. Alternative Investments: Explore alternative investments, such as real estate or commodities, to diversify your portfolio and reduce correlation with traditional assets.

4. Sector Rotation: Rotate investments into sectors that historically perform well during economic slowdowns, such as consumer staples or healthcare.

5. Cash Allocation: Maintain a strategic allocation to cash to capitalize on future opportunities that may arise during market corrections.

Contraction: Managing Debt, Cost Cutting, and Portfolio Preservation

During the contraction phase of the financial cycle, economic challenges and uncertainties come to the forefront. Businesses and individuals need to adopt strategies that focus on managing debt, cutting costs, and preserving their investment portfolios. Navigating this phase requires a disciplined and proactive approach. Here are strategies for managing your financial situation during the contraction phase:

Managing Debt:

1. Debt Prioritization: Identify high-interest debt and prioritize paying it off to reduce financial strain and interest payments.

2. Negotiation: Reach out to lenders to explore options for loan restructuring, temporary payment adjustments, or interest rate reductions.

3. Consolidation: Consider consolidating high-interest debts into a lower-interest loan to simplify payments and reduce overall interest costs.

4. Credit Utilization: Aim to reduce credit card and other unsecured debt by focusing on essential expenses and minimizing discretionary spending.

Cost Cutting:

1. Budget Revision: Review and revise your budget to focus on essential expenses, trimming non-essential spending to conserve resources.

2. Expense Prioritization: Differentiate between needs and wants, prioritizing necessary expenditures such as housing, utilities, and healthcare.

3. Negotiating Contracts: Negotiate with service providers, vendors, and suppliers for potential cost reductions or flexible payment terms.

4. Operational Efficiency: Streamline business operations and processes to reduce overhead costs and improve overall efficiency.

Portfolio Preservation:

1. Asset Review: Assess your investment portfolio and consider reallocating assets to more defensive positions, such as bonds or cash equivalents.

2. Diversification: Maintain a diversified portfolio to spread risk and reduce exposure to potential losses in specific sectors or industries.

3. Emergency Fund: Ensure you have an adequate emergency fund to cover essential expenses in case of unexpected income disruptions.

4. Professional Advice: Consult with financial advisors to evaluate your portfolio and receive guidance on potential adjustments based on your risk tolerance and goals.

5. Long-Term Focus: Stay focused on your long-term investment objectives and avoid making impulsive decisions driven by short-term market fluctuations.

6. Tax Efficiency: Explore tax-efficient investment strategies that minimize tax liabilities and preserve more of your investment returns.

7. Stay informed: Continuously monitor economic indicators, market trends, and policy developments that could impact your investments.

Through: Seizing Opportunities, Rebuilding, and Portfolio Diversification

During the trough phase of the financial cycle, the economy begins to stabilize and recover from the depths of the contraction. It's a critical time to seize opportunities, rebuild financial strength, and strategically position your investment portfolio for future growth. Here are strategies to consider during the trough phase:

Seizing Opportunities:

1. Asset Bargains: Look for undervalued assets in sectors that were hit hardest during the contraction phase, as they may offer attractive buying opportunities.

2. Equity Investments: Consider selectively investing in stocks of fundamentally strong companies with growth potential as they emerge from the downturn.

3. Real Estate: Explore real estate investments in areas where property values have been affected, aiming to benefit from potential appreciation during the recovery.

4. Acquisitions: For businesses, consider acquisitions or partnerships with distressed but viable companies that can enhance your market position.

Rebuilding:

1. Emergency Fund Replenishment: If your emergency fund was depleted during the recession, prioritize rebuilding it to provide a financial safety net.

2. Debt Repayment: Focus on reducing outstanding debt and improving your credit profile, which can strengthen your financial position.

3. Job Transition: Leverage the recovery to explore new job opportunities or career shifts that align with emerging market trends.

Portfolio Diversification:

1. Asset Allocation Review: Reassess your asset allocation to ensure it aligns with your risk tolerance and long-term goals.

2. Diversification: Maintain a diversified portfolio across different asset classes and geographic regions to spread risk and capture various growth opportunities.

3. Defensive Assets: While pursuing growth opportunities, ensure you still hold a portion of defensive assets, such as bonds, to provide stability.

4. Long-Term Investments: Consider allocating a portion of your portfolio to long-term investments with growth potential, aiming to capitalize on the recovery.

5. Rebalancing: Regularly rebalance your portfolio to ensure it remains aligned with your target asset allocation as market conditions evolve.

6. Professional Guidance: Consult with financial advisors to assess your portfolio, identify suitable investment options, and receive personalized advice based on your circumstances.

7. Patience: Understand that recovery is a gradual process, and it may take time for investments to fully realize their potential.

Chapter Four

Case Studies: Learning from Historical Financial Cycles

Certainly, analyzing past financial cycles may give significant insights into how different tactics and choices have played out in various economic conditions. Let's study a number of case studies that illustrate lessons learned from prior financial cycles:

Case Study 1:

The Great Recession (2007-2009)

The Great Recession was a significant worldwide economic crisis sparked by the collapse of the housing market and banking institutions. Many good lessons may be gleaned from this period:

1. Lesson: Overleveraging may lead to calamity.

During the pre-recession growth, many people and organizations accrued excessive debt, including subprime mortgages and complicated financial derivatives.

Result: When the housing bubble burst, overleveraged companies encountered insurmountable hurdles, leading to widespread defaults and financial instability.

2. Lesson: Risk assessment and openness are important.

Financial institutions possess complex and poorly understood assets, making it difficult to estimate risk exposure.

Result: Lack of openness and inadequate risk assessment contributed to the severity of the crisis and weakened market trust.

3. Lesson: Diversification and risk management are key.

Investors who significantly focused their holdings on real estate incurred big losses.

Result: Diversified portfolios performed better throughout the crisis, demonstrating the significance of risk management and diversification.

Case Study 2:

Dot-com Bubble (Late 1990s–Early 2000s)

The Dot-com Bubble was characterized by excessive speculation and quick price gains by technology companies, followed by a severe market decline.

1. Lesson: Avoid speculative bubbles and unreasonable excitement.

During the dot-com boom, investors were motivated by hype rather than fundamental prices.

Result: When the bubble broke, many overpriced firms faced bankruptcy, and investors incurred huge losses.

2. Lesson: Fundamental analysis is key.

Many IT businesses had interesting concepts but lacked solid business structures.

Result: Companies with strong foundations and effective business strategies were more likely to endure the crisis.

3. Lesson: Long-term perspective is crucial.

Investors who concentrated on short-term returns and neglected firm fundamentals incurred large losses.

Result: A long-term investment strategy, anchored on good research and analysis, was more successful.

4. Lesson: Valuation matters.

Companies with sky-high values were especially susceptible to declines.

Result: Investors learned the necessity of appraising a company's valuation compared to its profits and growth potential.

The Roaring Twenties and the Great Depression constitute a historic time of economic and financial extremes in the United States. Here's an overview of both eras:

The Roaring Twenties (1920–1929):

1. Economic Boom: Following World War I, the United States enjoyed a period of fast economic expansion, industrialization, and urbanization.

2. Consumption and Innovation: Technological developments and mass manufacturing led to increasing consumer spending and broad acceptance of new items like vehicles and radios.

3. Speculation and Stock Market Boom: The stock market witnessed a spectacular increase in the 1920s, with speculative purchasing pushing up share values.

4. Credit Expansion: Easy access to credit and payment plans encouraged many Americans to make purchases beyond their immediate means.

5. Crash of 1929: The stock market plummeted in October 1929, leading to a catastrophic economic crisis.

The Great Depression (1929–1940s):

1. Economic Collapse: The fall of 1929 heralded the beginning of the Great Depression, a time of significant economic contraction, widespread unemployment, and poverty.

2. Bank Failures: The financial sector experienced massive failures as banks failed, resulting in a severe credit crisis and decreased access to capital.

3. Dust Bowl: A severe drought in the Midwest led to agricultural destruction, further compounding economic problems.

4. Government Interventions: The New Deal was adopted by President Franklin D. Roosevelt and consisted of a series of measures meant to bring relief, economic recovery, and social revolution.

5. Market Regulation: The U.S. government introduced regulatory measures, notably the Glass-Steagall Act, to curb the excesses and risk-taking that led to the crisis.

6. Worldwide Impact: The Great Depression had a worldwide influence, resulting in diminished international commerce and economic suffering in many nations.

Key Lessons and Takeaways:

1. Speculative Excesses: The Roaring Twenties illustrated the hazards of unbridled speculation and market exuberance, which may lead to unsustainable asset bubbles.

2. Regulation and Intervention: The Great Depression underlined the necessity for robust financial regulation and government action during times of crisis to stabilize the economy and safeguard people.

3. Sustainable development: The experiences of both periods underline the significance of sustainable economic development, appropriate lending procedures, and avoiding undue debt.

4. Long-Term view: Investors should keep a long-term view, concentrating on sound fundamentals rather than short-term market volatility.

5. Balancing Growth: A balance between economic growth and appropriate risk management is vital to prevent excesses that might lead to catastrophic downturns.

The Roaring Twenties and the Great Depression serve as historical reminders of the possible repercussions of economic exuberance, speculative bubbles, and poor regulatory control. These lessons continue to shape economic policy and investment strategies to this day.

The Dot-Com Bubble and the Early 2000s Recession were major events in the world of finance and economics. Let's dig into each of these periods:

Dot-Com Bubble (Late 1990s–Early 2000s):

1. Technology Hype: During the late 1990s, there was a fast expansion of internet-based enterprises, many of which were speculative and had viable business plans.

2. Stock Market Surge: Investors raced to invest in these tech businesses, pushing up stock values to unsustainable heights despite many of these companies having little to no profitability.

3. Irrational Exuberance: The market became characterized by irrational excitement, with investors rejecting established valuation standards and pursuing any firm with a ".com" in its name.

4. Collapse: The bubble burst in 2000, when many overheated technology companies saw their values collapse. Many dot-com enterprises went out of business, and investors incurred huge losses.

Early 2000s Recession:

1. Economic Slowdown: The bust of the Dot-Com Bubble, along with corporate accounting scandals (e.g., Enron), led to an economic slowdown in the early 2000s.

2. Stock Market Decline: Stock markets dropped, resulting in lower consumer and business confidence. The S&P 500 Index had a protracted period of decline.

3. Global Impact: The U.S. recession had a worldwide influence, impacting economies in different areas, including Europe and Asia.

4. Monetary and Fiscal Policy: The Federal Reserve enacted interest rate reductions to boost the economy, while the U.S. government approved tax cuts to promote consumer spending.

Key Lessons and Takeaways:

1. Valuation Matters: The Dot-Com Bubble serves as a reminder of the necessity of analyzing the intrinsic worth of enterprises and avoiding speculative bubbles.

2. Business Fundamentals: Investors learned that even in the technology industry, good business fundamentals and sustainable growth models are necessary for long-term success.

3. Cautious Optimism: The early 2000s recession underlines the necessity for prudence and effective risk management even during times of economic prosperity.

4. Market Corrections: Both instances underscore the cyclical nature of markets and the significance of being prepared for market corrections and downturns.

5. Regulatory Oversight: Regulatory authorities and governments typically react to financial crises by taking steps to promote openness, reporting, and accountability.

6. Diversification: A diversified portfolio that covers several industries and asset classes may help lessen the effect of market downturns.

The Dot-Com Bubble and the Early 2000s Recession highlight how market exuberance, speculative behavior, and economic problems may affect financial markets and the wider economy. Learning from these occurrences may help investors and policymakers make more educated choices and foster more stable and sustainable economic development.

The Global Financial Crisis of 2008 was a landmark event that had far-reaching ramifications for the global economy and financial markets. Let's study the crisis and its aftermath:

Global Financial Crisis (2008):

1. Subprime Mortgage Crisis: The crisis was caused by the collapse of the U.S. housing market, led by the fall of the subprime mortgage bubble. Many homeowners defaulted on their mortgages, leading to severe financial difficulty.

2. Credit Freeze: Financial institutions owned complicated, mortgage-backed securities whose value fell. This led to a standstill in credit markets as banks were unwilling to lend to each other due to uncertainty about the size of their liabilities.

3. Lehman Brothers Collapse: The failure of Lehman Brothers in September 2008 intensified the crisis, producing fear and a loss of trust in financial markets.

4. Global Impact: The crisis swiftly extended throughout the world, resulting in a severe recession in many nations, stock market falls, and a global contraction of credit.

Aftermath and Lessons Learned:

1. Government Interventions: Governments throughout the globe intervened to stabilize financial markets and avert a full collapse of the banking sector. Measures included bank rescues, interest rate reductions, and stimulus programs.

2. Regulatory Reforms

The financial rules were reevaluated in reaction to the crisis. To enhance financial governance and minimize systemic risks, the Dodd-Frank Wall Street Reform and Consumer Protection Act was enacted in the United States.

3. Credit Tightening: Banks and financial institutions grew more cautious about lending, resulting in tighter credit conditions for households and companies.

4. Long-Term Impact on the Economy: The global economy endured a lengthy recovery phase, typified by weak growth, high unemployment rates, and issues in the housing and labor markets.

5. Impact on the Investment Landscape: Investors grew increasingly risk-averse and focused on the necessity of due diligence and risk assessment. Asset allocation and portfolio diversification gained fresh relevance.

6. Central Bank Policies: Central banks implemented unorthodox monetary policies, including quantitative easing, to encourage economic development and support financial markets.

7. Global Coordination: International collaboration and coordination among governments and central banks were vital in resolving the crisis and averting a more catastrophic result.

Key Lessons and Takeaways:

1. Risk Assessment: The crisis underlined the significance of appropriate risk assessment and transparency, especially in complex financial products.

2. Liquidity and Credit Risk: The crisis underlined the necessity of liquidity and the possibility of contagion in credit markets.

3. Systemic Risk Control: Effective supervision and control of systemic risks are crucial to sustaining financial stability.

4. Regulatory Oversight: Regulatory measures and tighter monitoring are needed to avoid excessive risk-taking and guarantee market integrity.

5. Global Interconnectedness: The crisis showed the interrelated nature of the global financial system and the necessity for international collaboration in handling crises.

The Global Financial Crisis of 2008 and its aftermath serve as a warning of the possible repercussions of unregulated risk-taking and the significance of cautious financial management, regulatory changes, and international cooperation in ensuring a stable and resilient global economy.

Chapter Five

Behavioral Finance and the Financial Cycle

Behavioral finance investigates how psychological and cognitive biases impact financial choices, especially those made throughout various parts of the financial cycle. Here's how behavioral finance overlaps with the financial cycle:

1. Expansion Phase:

Overconfidence: During periods of economic expansion, people could feel too optimistic about their investment choices, leading to excessive risk-taking.

Herding Behavior: As markets rise, the fear of losing out might lead investors to follow the throng, possibly contributing to asset bubbles.

Confirmation Bias: People prefer to seek information that supports their previous opinions, which may lead to disregarding warning indicators and overestimating the sustainability of development.

2. Peak Phase:

Loss Aversion: As markets peak, the fear of losing gains may encourage investors to hang on to assets longer than they should, missing chances to lock in profits. -

Over optimism: Overestimating the possibility of future gains might result in keeping hazardous investments even when values are stretched.

3. Contraction Phase:

Panic Selling: Fear and panic may push investors to sell assets at high losses during downturns, frequently resulting in illogical decision-making. **Loss Aversion:** The sensitivity to losses can discourage people from rearranging portfolios, leading to additional drops in riskier assets.

4. Trough Phase:

Recency Bias: The inclination to concentrate on recent events might cause investors to predict ongoing low performance, overlooking prospects for recovery.

Behavioral Biases: Psychological constraints may impair investors' ability to embrace chances in discounted assets, particularly after incurring losses.

5. Behavioral Strategies:

Education and Awareness: Recognizing behavioral biases may help people make more sensible judgments, especially during emotional market cycles.

Goal-Based Investing: Setting defined financial goals might help investors make choices based on long-term goals rather than short-term emotions.

Automation: Implementing automated investing techniques, such as monthly contributions to retirement accounts, helps overcome emotional biases.

Investor Sentiment: Greed, Fear, and Market Psychology

Investor sentiment has a crucial impact on determining market dynamics and driving asset values. It generally swings between two major emotional states: greed and terror. Understanding market psychology and how these emotions impact investor behavior is vital for navigating the financial cycle. Here's how greed, anxiety, and market psychology affect investing decisions:

1. Greed:

Excessive Optimism: Greed emerges as excessive optimism about market prospects and possible profits on investments.

Risk-Taking: Investors motivated by greed could seek out high-risk investments in the quest for rapid returns.

Speculative Bubbles: Greed may lead to the emergence of asset bubbles when investors bid up prices without proper consideration of underlying fundamentals.

Herd Mentality: In moments of greed, investors prefer to follow the pack, afraid they will miss out on rich opportunities.

Overleveraging: Greedy conduct may lead to borrowing beyond one's means to enhance prospective benefits.

2. Fear:

Excessive pessimism: Fear leads to negative outlooks on markets and the economy, typically underestimating recovery possibilities.

Sell-Offs and Panic: Fear-driven selling during market falls may lead to significant price decreases and greater volatility.

Safe Haven Assets: Investors seek sanctuary in safe-haven assets, such as gold or government bonds, during times of fear and uncertainty.

Loss Aversion: Fear of losing money may lead to hesitation in making investing choices, resulting in wasted chances.

Short-Term Focus: Fear-driven actions tend to favor short-term safety above long-term development potential.

3. Market Psychology:

Behavioral Biases: Cognitive biases, such as overconfidence, confirmation bias, and recency bias, impact investment judgments.

Contrarian chances: Market psychology generates chances for contrarian investors who purchase when fear is strong and sell when greed prevails.

Sentiment Indicators: Analysts employ sentiment indicators, such as the CBOE Volatility Index (VIX) or surveys, to evaluate investor mood and anticipate market changes.

Feedback Loop: Investor mood may produce self-reinforcing cycles where fear begets more selling and greed leads to greater purchasing.

4. Navigating Investor Sentiment:

Emotional Discipline: Recognize emotional biases and make investing choices based on logical analysis rather than short-term emotions.

Diversification: Maintain a diversified portfolio to lessen the influence of significant sentiment movements on overall performance.

Long-Term Perspective: Focus on long-term investing objectives and avoid making hasty choices based on short-term market swings.

Contrarian Approach: Consider contrarian methods that entail purchasing inexpensive assets during moments of fear and selling overpriced assets during periods of greed.

Education and Awareness: Stay knowledgeable on market psychology, behavioral biases, and historical market cycles to make informed judgments.

Herd Mentality and Cognitive Biases

Herd mentality and cognitive biases are two psychological phenomena that strongly impact individual and group decision-making, frequently leading to patterns of behavior that may not be rational or optimal. Here's a deeper look at each of these concepts:

1. Herd Mentality:

Two psychological phenomena, herd mentality and cognitive biases, have a substantial influence on individual and collective decision-making, often resulting in patterns of behavior that may not be ideal or rational. Let's analyze each of these principles in greater detail:

Fear of Missing Out (FOMO): Investors may dread losing out on prospective returns, pushing them to invest in growing trends or speculative assets without sufficient examination.

Social affirmation: People seek affirmation from others and feel that if many are doing something, it must be the appropriate course of action.

Lack of Information: When unsure, people typically seek the behaviors of others for direction, thinking that the collective must hold greater information.

Amplification of Trends: Herd behavior may magnify both upward and negative market trends, leading to the emergence of bubbles and collapses.

2. Cognitive Biases:

Cognitive biases, which typically emerge from mental heuristics or defects in the way information is processed, are recurring patterns of judgmental departure from the norm or reason. These biases may result in erroneous judgments and decisions. Cognitive biases may have an influence on investment choices and behavior in the realm of finance. A few important biases are:

Confirmation Bias: People prefer to seek and interpret information that supports their prior opinions, dismissing contrary data.

Overconfidence Bias: Individuals overestimate their own talents and expertise, leading to excessive risk-taking or refusal to consider alternate opinions.

Anchoring Bias: When forming judgments, individuals have a propensity to put too much weight on the first piece of information they come across, even if it is untrustworthy or out-of-date.

Loss Aversion: The fear of losing is bigger than the joy of earning, prompting investors to cling on to failing assets longer than they should.

Recency Bias: People assign greater weight to recent occurrences, expecting that current patterns will continue into the future.

➤ Impact on Financial Decisions:

Herd mentality and cognitive biases may greatly impact financial choices, frequently leading to irrational behavior and market inefficiencies.

Market Bubbles and Crashes: Herd behavior may lead to the emergence of asset bubbles (e.g., the Dot-Com Bubble) and sudden market collapses (e.g., the 2008 Financial Crisis).

Overreaction and Underreaction: Cognitive biases may lead to an overreaction to news or events, creating exaggerated price swings. Conversely, underreaction may delay responsiveness to new information.

Missed Opportunities: Cognitive biases may lead to lost investment opportunities due to a failure to examine important information or other opinions.

Suboptimal Portfolios: Investors affected by herd behavior and prejudices may wind up with suboptimal portfolios that may not correspond with their risk tolerance and long-term objectives.

> **Managing Herd Mentality and Cognitive Biases:**

Education: Understand and learn about typical cognitive biases and their influence on decision-making to make better-informed decisions.

Independent study: Base judgments on careful study and research rather than mindlessly following the herd.

Long-Term Focus: Maintain a long-term investing perspective and avoid making hasty judgments prompted by short-term trends or emotions.

Diversification: Build a diversified portfolio to limit the influence of herd behavior and individual biases on overall investing performance.

Professional Guidance: Seek guidance from financial specialists who can give objective views and help avoid emotional biases.

Emotional Intelligence in Investment Decision-Making

Emotional intelligence (EI) refers to the capacity to identify, comprehend, regulate, and successfully utilize emotions in ourselves and others. In the context of investment decision-making, emotional intelligence plays a vital role in helping investors make reasonable and well-informed decisions, manage risk, and accomplish long-term financial objectives. Here's how emotional intelligence affects investment decision-making:

1. Self-Awareness:

Recognizing Feelings: Investors with high emotional intelligence can detect their own feelings, such as fear, greed, or enthusiasm, that may affect their decision-making.

Impact on Decisions: Being aware of emotional biases helps investors avoid making impulsive or unreasonable choices motivated by short-term emotions.

2.Self-Regulation:

Managing Impulsivity: Emotional intelligence helps investors regulate impulsive behavior that may lead to purchasing high and selling cheap.

Coping with Losses: Investors with EI can absorb losses better, avoiding panic selling during market downturns.

3. Empathy:

Understanding Market Sentiment: Empathy helps investors comprehend the collective feelings of the market and make educated judgments.

Anticipating Trends: Empathetic investors can forecast how the market mood could evolve and modify their strategy appropriately.

4. Social Skills:

Effective Communication: Emotional intelligence promotes communication with financial advisers, peers, and specialists, leading to better-informed judgments.

Collaborative Learning: Investors with EI may learn from others' experiences by adopting effective techniques and avoiding common traps.

5. Decision-Making:

Balancing Emotions and Analysis: EI helps investors establish a balance between emotional impulses and intellectual analysis when making investing choices.

Long-Term Perspective: Emotional intelligence fosters a focus on long-term objectives, decreasing the influence of short-term market swings.

6. Coping with Market Turbulence:

Staying Cool: Emotional intelligence helps investors be cool and collected amid market turbulence, avoiding knee-jerk responses.

Opportunistic Mindset: EI helps investors perceive market downturns as opportunities rather than dangers, uncovering undervalued assets.

7. Risk Management:

Assessing Risk Tolerance: Emotional intelligence helps investors properly measure their risk tolerance and make investing decisions consistent with their comfort levels.

Controlling Fear and Greed: EI supports controlling emotions like fear and greed that may lead to excessive risk-taking or avoidance of chances.

8. Continuous Learning:

Adapting to Change: Emotional intelligence increases flexibility, enabling investors to modify tactics depending on changing market circumstances.

Learning from Mistakes: EI facilitates learning from prior failures, reducing repeat errors.

Chapter Six

Future Trends and Technological Impacts on the Financial Cycle

The financial sector is facing dramatic changes spurred by technological developments and emerging trends. These innovations are projected to have a dramatic influence on the financial cycle, altering how economic stages unfold and how organizations and people navigate them. Here are some future trends and technology implications to consider:

1. Digitalization and Fintech:

Digital Payments and Banking: The move toward digital payments and online banking is anticipated to continue, impacting the way transactions are done and financial services are accessed.

Fintech Innovation: Fintech startups are challenging conventional financial services by delivering novel solutions for lending, investing, and risk management.

2. Artificial Intelligence (AI) and Machine Learning:

Automated Decision-Making: AI-powered algorithms may boost investment decisions, risk assessment, and portfolio management, leading to more efficient and data-driven choices.

Fraud Detection: AI can increase fraud detection and prevention, boosting security measures inside financial transactions.

3. Blockchain and Cryptocurrencies:

Decentralized Finance (DeFi):

Blockchain technology facilitates the emergence of decentralized financial services, possibly disrupting conventional banking and lending patterns.

Digital Assets: Cryptocurrencies and digital tokens may become increasingly integrated into investing plans, asset management, and international transactions.

4. Big Data and Analytics:

Predictive Analytics: The capacity to analyze enormous volumes of data may lead to more accurate economic projections, helping investors and companies plan for fluctuations in the financial cycle.

Customized Financial Services: Big data may allow financial organizations to deliver customized services suited to specific consumer demands.

5. Regulatory Technology (RegTech):

Compliance and Risk Management: RegTech solutions improve regulatory compliance procedures while cutting costs and boosting transparency in financial activities.

6. Sustainable Finance:

Environmental, Social, and Governance (ESG) Investing:

The trend toward sustainable investing is projected to continue, impacting investment choices and company policies.

7. Cybersecurity:

Data Protection: As financial transactions and services become increasingly computerized, cybersecurity measures will be important to secure sensitive financial information.

8. Globalization and Geopolitics:

Cross-Border Transactions: Technological improvements may promote cross-border commerce and investment, altering global economic patterns.

Geopolitical Risks: The interconnection of financial institutions may lead to heightened vulnerability to geopolitical events.

9. Automation and the Future of Work:

Impact on Jobs: Automation and AI might redefine employment responsibilities within the financial industry, pushing individuals to adapt and gain new skills.

10. Quantum Computing:

Advanced Data Processing: Quantum computing has the potential to revolutionize data processing and complicated financial modeling, providing solutions not achievable with traditional computing.

Digital Disruption: Fintech, Blockchain, and Cryptocurrencies:

Digital disruption in the financial sector, fueled by fintech, blockchain technology, and cryptocurrencies, is transforming how financial services are supplied, transactions are done, and assets are maintained. Here's a deeper look at each of these factors and their impact:

1. Fintech (Financial Technology):

Definition: Fintech refers to technology-driven innovations that strive to enhance and automate financial services, from payments and lending to wealth management and insurance.

Impact: Fintech challenges conventional financial services, making them more accessible, efficient, and customer-centric. Examples: peer-to-peer lending systems, robo-advisors, mobile payment applications, and digital wallets.

2. Blockchain Technology:

Definition: Blockchain is a decentralized and secure digital ledger that records transactions across several computers. It provides openness, immutability, and data integrity.

Impact: Blockchain promotes trust, removes middlemen, and allows safe and efficient peer-to-peer transactions.

Use Cases: Cross-border payments, supply chain management, identity verification, and smart contracts

3. Cryptocurrencies:

Definition: Cryptocurrencies are characterized as digital or virtual money that is safeguarded by cryptography. Utilizing blockchain technology, they run.

Impact: Cryptocurrencies allow borderless, decentralized transactions, financial inclusion, and the capacity to serve as a store of wealth. Stablecoins, Ripple, Ethereum, and Bitcoin are a few examples.

4. Disruption and Transformation:

Conventional Banking: Fintech challenges conventional banks by delivering digital banking services, speedier transactions, and enhanced client experiences.

Remittances: Blockchain and cryptocurrencies simplify cross-border remittances, cutting costs and transaction times.

Financial Inclusion: Fintech and cryptocurrencies enable access to financial services for unbanked and underbanked communities.

Decentralization: Blockchain's decentralized nature decreases the need for middlemen and fosters confidence in transactions.

5. Challenges and Considerations:

Regulatory Environment: Fintech and cryptocurrencies confront developing regulatory frameworks that differ by country.

Security: Blockchain and cryptocurrencies must address security issues, including hacking and fraud threats.

Volatility: Cryptocurrencies' price volatility offers investing and payment issues.

Integration: Traditional financial institutions must adapt and incorporate fintech technologies to stay competitive.

6. Innovation and Collaboration:

Partnerships: Traditional financial institutions partner with fintech firms to develop and improve services.

Research and Development: Blockchain is researched for many applications, including supply chain traceability, real estate, and healthcare.

7. Future Possibilities:

Central Bank Digital Currencies (CBDCs): Governments consider releasing digital versions of their national currencies for increased payment efficiency.

Tokenization: Traditional assets, like real estate or equities, may be tokenized on the blockchain, permitting fractional ownership and liquidity.

Artificial Intelligence and Algorithmic Trading

Artificial Intelligence (AI) and algorithmic trading are two interrelated technologies that have changed the financial sector by automating and streamlining trading procedures. Here's a summary of both AI and algorithmic trading and their impact:

Artificial Intelligence (AI):

Definition: AI refers to the modeling of human cognitive processes by computers, including learning, reasoning, problem-solving, and decision-making.

Applications in Finance: AI is employed in different sectors of finance, including investment management, risk assessment, fraud detection, customer service, and trading. Machine learning is a field of artificial intelligence that comprises the use of algorithms that constantly improve as a consequence of data collection. Deep learning is a method of machine learning that incorporates neural networks and sophisticated data models.

Algorithmic Trading:

Definition: Algorithmic trading, often known as algo trading or automated trading, involves utilizing pre-programmed instructions to execute trade orders automatically.

Objectives: Algorithmic trading strives to enhance execution speed, accuracy, and efficiency while eliminating the effect of human emotions on trading choices.

Techniques: Algorithms may be constructed for different trading techniques, such as market making, arbitrage, trend tracking, and statistical arbitrage.

High-Frequency Trading (HFT): A subclass of algorithmic trading, HFT involves executing a large number of orders at very high speeds.

AI and Algorithmic Trading: AI can analyze enormous volumes of data and uncover patterns that people would ignore, enhancing the efficacy of algorithmic trading techniques.

Predictive Analytics: AI-driven algorithms can forecast market movements and pricing patterns based on historical data and real-time information.

Risk Management: AI can monitor market circumstances and change trading methods to control risks and limit losses.

Adaptability: AI-powered algorithms may adapt their approach in reaction to changing market conditions.

High-Speed Decision-Making: AI-driven algorithmic trading systems are able to make trades in a matter of milliseconds, seizing the moment.

Benefits:

Efficiency: Algorithmic trading lowers human involvement, resulting in quicker execution and decreased transaction costs.

Consistency: Algorithms obey set rules consistently, minimizing emotional biases that might impair human traders.

Diversification: Algorithms may monitor and trade across many markets and assets concurrently, achieving superior diversification.

Backtesting: Algorithms may be tested on previous data to determine their performance before deployment.

Liquidity Provision: Algorithmic traders may supply liquidity to markets, decreasing bid-ask spreads.

Challenges and Considerations:

Data Quality: Accurate and timely data is vital for AI-driven algorithmic trading.

Model Overfitting: Algorithms may perform well on past data but struggle with fresh market circumstances.

Regulatory Compliance: Algorithmic trading must comply with regulatory norms and risk management processes.

Sustainable Finance and ESG Investing

Sustainable finance and ESG (Environmental, Social, and Governance) investment are fast-growing movements in the financial sector that emphasize not just financial returns but also good social and environmental consequences. Here's an outline of sustainable finance and ESG investing:

1. Sustainable Finance:

Definition: Sustainable finance refers to the integration of environmental, social, and governance (ESG) elements into financial decision-making processes.

Objectives: The purpose of sustainable finance is to encourage long-term value generation, support ecologically responsible behaviors, and contribute to social well-being.

Key Components: Sustainable finance covers many methodologies, such as ESG investment, impact investing, green bonds, and corporate social responsibility (CSR).

2. ESG Investing:

Environmental (E): Focuses on a company's influence on the environment, including elements such as carbon emissions, resource utilization, and pollution.

Social (S): Examines a company's interactions with workers, communities, and other stakeholders, examining problems like labor practices, diversity, and community participation.

Governance (G): Assesses a company's corporate governance framework, transparency, accountability, and ethical conduct.

Impact of Sustainable Finance and ESG Investing:

Investor Demand: Growing awareness of environmental and social concerns has led to a growing demand for investments that align with investors' beliefs.

Risk Management: Companies with high ESG performance are frequently better positioned to handle risks, such as legislative changes and reputational harm.

Long-Term Value: ESG variables may contribute to a company's long-term financial success and resiliency.

Regulatory Drivers: Governments and regulatory organizations are developing regulations that promote ESG disclosure and incorporation into investing practices.

Stakeholder Engagement: ESG considerations build stronger interactions with stakeholders, including consumers, workers, and communities.

Sustainable Finance Instruments:

ESG Integration: Incorporating ESG issues into investing analysis and decision-making.

Thematic investing: Investing in topics such as renewable energy, sustainable technology, and social impact.

Impact Investing: Allocating money to produce beneficial social and environmental consequences with financial profits.

Green Bonds: Bonds issued to support projects with special environmental advantages, such as renewable energy projects or clean water efforts.

Social Bonds: Similar to green bonds but focused on social projects like affordable housing or education programs.

Challenges and Considerations:

Data Quality and Standardization: ESG data might be inconsistent or absent, making it tough to compare organizations' performance.

Measurement and measurements: Determining the influence of ESG issues on financial performance may be challenging and requires defined measurements.

Greenwashing: Some firms may make misleading or exaggerated claims about their ESG initiatives, highlighting the need for openness and accountability.

<u>Chapter Seven</u>

Building Resilience in Your Financial Journey

Building financial resilience is vital for handling life's uncertainties, economic changes, and unforeseen occurrences. It entails adopting tactics and behaviors that help you resist financial problems and recover from failures. Here are crucial strategies to establish resilience in your financial journey:

1. Emergency Fund:

Build and manage an emergency fund with 3 to 6 months' worth of living costs. This fund offers a safety net for unexpected occurrences like medical emergencies or job losses.

2. Planning and Budgeting:

Establish a detailed budget to keep an eye on profits and outlays. Prioritize saving for significant expenditures and long-term needs by defining financial targets.

3. Debt management:

Avoid high-interest debt and make a determined effort to pay off your present commitments in a timely manner. Prioritize paying off your commitments in order to lower interest rates.

4. Diversified Investments:

Diversify your investment portfolio across numerous asset classes and businesses. This decreases risk and helps your portfolio survive market changes.

5. Insurance Coverage:

Ensure you have appropriate health, life, disability, and property insurance. Insurance protects you from severe financial losses due to unforeseen circumstances.

6. Constant Learning: Maintain your understanding of personal finance and investment methods. Making knowledgeable choices and reacting to evolving financial conditions are made feasible through constant learning.

7. Living Below Your Means:

Avoid overspending and focus on living below your means. This enables you to save and invest for the future while maintaining financial security.

8. Flexibility and adaptability:

Be prepared to change your financial strategies in response to changing circumstances. Adaptability helps you negotiate unforeseen circumstances with resilience.

9. Long-Term Perspective:

Focus on long-term financial objectives rather than short-term market volatility. A long-term view lowers the influence of emotional responses to market volatility.

10. Seeking Professional Advice:

Consult financial professionals for tailored assistance on investing, retirement planning, and tax strategies.

11. Mental and Emotional Resilience:

Develop appropriate coping methods to handle stress and emotions associated with financial issues.

12. Estate Planning:

Create a will and prepare an estate plan to guarantee your assets are transferred according to your intentions.

13. Networking and Support:

Build a network of supportive friends, family, and mentors who can give direction and emotional support.

14. Self-Care:

Prioritize self-care to preserve physical and emotional well-being, which favorably influences your capacity to handle funds.

Long-Term Financial Planning and Goal Setting

Long-term financial planning entails identifying defined financial objectives and building a detailed strategy to attain those goals over an extended period. Proper long-term planning gives you a path to manage your money, grow wealth, and work toward your ambitions. Here's a step-by-step method for successful long-term financial planning and goal setting:

1. Define Your Financial Goals:

Define your financial goals, both long-term and short-term. Debt repayment is an example of a short-term ambition, while a long-term target might be retirement or purchasing a property.

2. Prioritize Your Goals:

Rank your financial objectives based on their relevance and duration. This lets you deploy resources efficiently.

3. Set Specific and Measurable goals:

Define each aim with accuracy. For example, if your objective is to retire comfortably, define the age at which you hope to retire and the income you wish to achieve.

4. Quantify Your Goals:

Assign a financial number or numerical value to your objectives. This helps you establish a realistic savings and investment strategy.

5. Create a Budget:

Create a complete budget that includes a breakdown of your income, outgoing expenses, and savings. Maintaining a budget helps you keep tabs on your financial status and make informed decisions.

6. Assess Your Current Financial Situation:

Evaluate your present assets, obligations, income, and spending. Understanding your financial situation provides a framework for goal planning.

7. Develop a Savings and Investment Strategy:

Determine how much you need to save or invest consistently to attain your objectives. Consider numerous investing alternatives depending on your risk tolerance and time horizon.

8. Account for Inflation:

Factor in the effect of inflation on your objectives and assets. Adjust your financial estimates appropriately.

9. Retirement Planning:

Plan for retirement by estimating your planned retirement income and calculating the funds necessary to obtain that income.

10. Risk Management:

Purchase appropriate insurance coverage to defend against unforeseen occurrences that might jeopardize your financial ambitions.

11. Estate Planning:

Create a will, create trusts, and prepare for the disposal of your assets according to your preferences.

12. Regularly Review and adjust:

Periodically examine your financial objectives, analyze your progress, and make appropriate improvements to your strategy.

13. Seek Professional advice:

Consult financial experts, accountants, and legal specialists to verify that your long-term financial strategy corresponds with your objectives.

14. Stay Disciplined and patient:

Long-term financial planning needs discipline and patience. Stick to your goal even through market swings and life changes.

15. Monitor Tax efficiency:

Consider tax-efficient techniques to reduce tax payments and enhance your financial results.

Emergency Funds and Risk Management

Emergency savings and risk management are key components of a strong financial strategy. They offer you a safety net to manage unforeseen events and prevent possible financial losses. Here's a deeper look at emergency savings and risk management strategies:

1. Emergency Funds:

Definition: An emergency fund is a reserved sum of money put up to handle unforeseen costs or financial crises.

Purpose: Emergency savings offer a cushion that helps you avoid getting into debt or making hasty financial choices when unexpected occurrences strike.

Recommended Size: Maintain an emergency reserve with three to six months' worth of living expenses. Your circumstances will decide the actual amount.

Why Emergency Funds are Important:

Work Loss: If you lose your job, an emergency fund may cover your living costs while you look for new employment.

Medical Emergencies: Unforeseen medical bills may be covered without placing pressure on your finances.

Car or Home repairs: When unexpected repairs are required, your emergency fund may help pay the expenses.

Avoiding Debt: An emergency fund helps you avoid depending on credit cards or loans for unanticipated needs.

Risk Management Strategies:

Insurance Coverage: Adequate insurance coverage, including health, life, disability, and property insurance, defends you from financial loss due to unforeseen circumstances.

Diversified Investments: Diversifying your investment portfolio across several asset classes lessens the influence of market volatility on your overall financial situation.

Estate Planning: Creating a will and developing an estate plan guarantee that your assets are transferred according to your intentions.

Health and well-being: Maintaining excellent health and well-being decreases the chance of medical crises and related expenditures.

How to Create and Maintain an Emergency Fund

1. Set a Goal: Calculate how much you'll need to save to pay for three to six months' worth of expenditures.

2. Start Small: To start, put aside a portion of your monthly paycheck.

3. Automate Savings: Set up automatic payments to your emergency fund to maintain continuous contributions.

4. Avoid Temptation: Keep your emergency fund distinct from your usual spending accounts to prevent the temptation to utilize it for non-emergencies.

5. Regularly Review: Periodically examine your emergency fund's size to account for changes in your financial condition.

Risk Management Tips:

a. Consistently examine your insurance policies to make sure they are current and provide appropriate coverage.

b. Talk to a financial adviser to establish your risk tolerance and build a diversified investment strategy.

c. Update your estate plan if life circumstances change, such as marriage, children, or large asset purchases.

Continual Learning and Adaptability in Personal Finance

Continual learning and adaptation are crucial traits for effectively managing your personal money in an ever-changing economic and financial world. Staying educated, obtaining new information, and being open to adjusting your techniques are crucial to reaching your financial objectives. Here's how ongoing learning and flexibility contribute to your financial well-being:

1. Staying Informed:

Economic Trends: Understanding economic indicators and market trends helps you make educated judgments regarding investments and financial planning.

Regulatory Changes: Being informed of changes in tax laws, regulations, and financial policies helps you maximize your financial plans.

2. Evolving Financial Products:

Stay informed on new financial products, tools, and services that may improve your financial management and help you reach your objectives.

3. Investment Education:

Learn about numerous investing alternatives, risk management approaches, and ways to optimize returns while limiting risks.

4. Debt Management:

Continually educate yourself about effective debt management tactics, interest rates, and repayment alternatives to decrease debt effectively.

5. Technology and Automation:

Stay aware of technical innovations that may ease financial responsibilities, such as budgeting applications, investing platforms, and automated savings programs.

6. Adaptability:

Life Changes: Be prepared to adapt your financial goals when encountering life events such as marriage, children, professional changes, or unexpected spending.

Market Volatility: Adapt your investing methods in response to shifting market circumstances and economic upheavals.

7. Embracing New Opportunities:

Be open to researching new income streams, side hustles, or investment possibilities that correspond with your financial objectives.

8. Reducing Behavioral Biases:

Continual learning may help you discover and overcome typical behavioral biases that could impact your financial choices.

9. Seeking Professional Advice:

Consult financial planners, tax specialists, and other experts to get specific expertise and help.

10. Long-Term Perspective:

Continual learning helps you preserve a long-term perspective, reducing knee-jerk responses to short-term market changes.

11. Financial Literacy:

Improving your financial literacy boosts your capacity to handle your resources efficiently and make educated choices.

12. Personal Growth:

Continual learning and flexibility encourage personal development, self-confidence, and a feeling of empowerment in managing your money.

Conclusion

In conclusion, comprehending the complexity of the financial cycle and attaining long-term financial success demand a diversified strategy. From comprehending the economic stages of growth, peak, contraction, and trough to embracing the possibilities of technological innovations like fintech, blockchain, and cryptocurrencies, your path through the financial landscape is a dynamic and ever-evolving one.

Effective financial management entails not just the strategic allocation of resources but also a comprehensive grasp of investor mood, emotional intelligence, and behavioral biases that might impact decision-making. By adopting sustainable finance, ESG investment, and fostering resilience, you position yourself to weather risks and capitalize on opportunities while contributing positively to society and the environment.

Your dedication to ongoing learning, adaptation, and defining clear financial objectives acts as a compass, leading you through economic upheavals, personal milestones, and unanticipated problems. As you navigate this difficult route, remember that getting expert guidance, maintaining emergency reserves, and exercising risk management are important to your financial well-being.

Ultimately, your financial path reflects your objectives, principles, and devotion. By incorporating the ideas and techniques provided in this book, you empower yourself to make educated choices, safeguard your financial future, and begin on a road of sustained development and wealth. As you continue on this road, always remember that the quest for financial knowledge is a lifetime adventure, and your dedication to learning and adapting will serve as the cornerstone of your financial success.

Mastering the Financial Cycle: A Lifelong Pursuit

Embarking on the quest to manage the financial cycle is not a goal but rather a lifetime effort. The delicate dance of economic stages, market movements, and investor mood needs consistent attention to learning, adjusting, and making educated judgments. Just as the financial world develops, so must our understanding and strategy.

From comprehending the intricacies of growth and contraction to leveraging the potential of cutting-edge technology like AI and blockchain, each step in the journey presents possibilities to develop and prosper. The books of history, with their accounts of economic booms and disasters, provide vital insights that lead us through present issues.

Sustainable finance and ESG investment remind us that our financial actions have larger effects. By aligning our portfolios with our principles, we contribute to good change and influence the world we foresee. At the same time, the concepts of resilience and adaptation prepare us for the unpredictable, helping us weather storms and grab chances for change.

As we negotiate the financial cycle, we come face-to-face with our own tendencies and prejudices. Emotional intelligence and a balanced viewpoint become our partners in making reasonable decisions, remaining grounded at market highs, and being patient during lows.

Above all, this aim is one of ongoing progress. Our financial journey is not simply about amassing riches; it is also about increasing our knowledge, widening our views, and developing power over the forces that drive our economies and our lives. In this endeavor, we discover empowerment, stability, and the capacity to determine our own financial future.

So, let us commence this lifetime endeavor with open minds and resolute spirits. Let us learn from the past, appreciate the present, and prepare for the future. As we master the financial cycle, we construct a path that leads to success, meaning, and a legacy of prudent financial management.